THE UNITED STATES PRESIDENTS

WILLIAM
CLINTON

OUR 42ND PRESIDENT

by Ann Graham Gaines

childsworld.com

1980 Lookout Drive • Mankato, MN 56003-1705
800-599-READ • www.childsworld.com

ACKNOWLEDGMENTS
Content Adviser: David R. Smith, Adjunct Assistant
Professor of History, University of Michigan–Ann Arbor

PHOTOS
Cover and page 3: Everett Collection/Newscom (detail)
Interior: akg-images/Newscom, 12; Andy Martin Jr./ZUMA Press/
Newscom, 36; Arnold Sachs/Archive Photos via Getty Images, 10;
Associated Press, 17, 20, 21, 24, 26, 28, 31, 32, 33, 34, 38 (bottom
left); CSU Archives/Everett Collection/Bridgeman Images, 18;
Dennis Brack bb51/Newscom, 27; Everett Collection/Bridgeman
Images, 16, 38 (right); Everett Collection/Newscom, 19; GARY
HERSHORN/REUTERS/Newscom, 25; Georges De Keerle/Hulton
Archive via Getty Images, 29; Hulton Archive via Getty Images, 7;
James Berglie/ZUMAPRESS/Newscom, 35, 39; Mathieu Polak/
Sygma via Getty Images, 11, 38 (top left); United States Senate
Via CNP/Newscom, 37; US National Archives and Records
Administration, 4, 22; US National Park Service, 5; Wellesley
College Archives, 14; William J. Clinton Presidential Library, 6, 9

ISBN 9781503844339 (REINFORCED LIBRARY BINDING)
ISBN 9781503847200 (PORTABLE DOCUMENT FORMAT)
ISBN 9781503848399 (ONLINE MULTI-USER EBOOK)
LCCN 2019958001

Printed in the United States of America

CONTENTS

President Bill Clinton
once said, "By lifting the
weakest, the poorest
among us, we lift the
rest of us as well."

CHAPTER ONE

ARKANSAS CHILDHOOD

William J. Clinton was the 42nd president of the United States. He served for two **terms,** from 1993 to 2001. Many Americans think Bill Clinton was a good president. They point to the fact that while Clinton was in office, the American **economy** was healthy. Many Americans had jobs that paid well, and the government was able to save some money.

However, President Clinton's reputation was damaged during his second term, when he was involved in a **scandal.** He was accused of dishonesty, and Congress brought **impeachment** proceedings against him. He became the second president in American history to be tried by Congress.

During the impeachment hearings, Clinton was **acquitted**—found not guilty of the charges against him. He stayed in office and finished his second term.

Bill Clinton did not have an easy childhood. He was determined to succeed, however, and worked hard to achieve his goals.

Bill Clinton spent his first years living at his grandparents' home (pictured) in Hope, Arkansas. His mother returned to school to study nursing, so his grandparents took care of him.

Bill Clinton was born on August 19, 1946, in Hope, a small town in southwestern Arkansas. His parents, Virginia and Bill Blythe, had married three years earlier. Bill Blythe then went off to fight in World War II. When he returned, the couple moved to Chicago, Illinois, where Bill had a job. Virginia, who was pregnant, went home for a time to Arkansas. While traveling back to Arkansas to pick her up, Bill Blythe was killed in a car accident.

After her husband died, Virginia Blythe stayed with her parents. Three months later, her baby was born. She named him William Jefferson Blythe, after his father, and nicknamed him "Billy."

When Billy was about a year old, Virginia asked her parents to take care of him. Before the war, she had worked as a nurse. She wanted to return to nursing school to learn new skills so she could earn more money. She knew she would need it to raise Billy by herself. Virginia studied to become a nurse **anesthetist,** which meant she would help give drugs to patients to prevent pain during surgery.

This photograph shows Clinton's grandfather, James Cassidy (on the right), in his grocery store in Hope, Arkansas.

Bill Clinton was the first president to be born after World War II.

Bill Clinton's grandparents were not well educated, but they knew the importance of learning. They taught Bill to count and read at a young age. In first grade, Bill was already reading the newspaper.

Bill lived with his grandparents for about two years. Years later, Bill Clinton would remember that although he missed his mother, her mother and father took good care of him. His grandfather James took him to work at his grocery store and to his second job, as a watchman at a sawmill. His grandmother cared for Bill at home. When he was still a very little boy, she started teaching him to read.

Virginia finished school in 1950. That same year, she remarried. Her new husband was a car salesman named Roger Clinton. Bill went to live with them. Sadly, it was not a very happy family. Roger was an alcoholic, which means he had a drinking problem. He and Virginia often had very angry arguments.

When Bill was seven years old, the family moved to the city of Hot Springs, Arkansas. There Bill got to know the rest of the Clintons, his stepfather's large family. He kept in touch with his grandparents, who moved away from Hope soon after their daughter did. In 1956, his family expanded, when his brother, Roger, was born. Years later, he'd remember that year fondly for a second reason—it was when the Clinton family bought their first television set. He loved the children's shows. He was also fascinated by the Democratic and Republican national conventions of 1956. The Democrats and the Republicans are the two most important political groups in the United States. In a presidential election year, each party holds a national convention to choose its **candidate** for president. Even in 1956, when Bill was only 10 years old, he was interested in what it takes for a person to become president of the United States.

Growing up, Billy Clinton was a friendly, outgoing boy. He is around four years old in this photograph.

7

By the time he was in high school, Bill Clinton had developed what would be lifelong interests. On his own, he had joined a church. Always a reader, he'd developed into an excellent student. He had learned to play the saxophone and joined the school band. He remained devoted to his mother and his brother, whom he tried to protect from his **abusive** step-father. A friendly boy, he was active and popular. His classmates elected him class president.

During the summer of 1963, Clinton felt honored when teachers at his high school selected him to go to Arkansas Boys State. The American Legion sponsors this special camp every year. Boys who attend learn about the government and hold their own elections. The other boys elected Bill a senator. With Boys State senators from all 50 states, he traveled to Washington, DC, to participate in Boys Nation. There the boys split into **political parties.** They discussed the important issues of the day. They also toured the Capitol, the Library of Congress, and other historic landmarks. The highlight of this trip for Bill Clinton occurred on July 24. That was the day all the boys were invited to the White House. There they posed for photographs with President John F. Kennedy. Bill Clinton made sure he was the first in line to shake President Kennedy's hand.

When he was 14, Bill Clinton officially took his stepfather's last name.

As a teenager, Bill loved the music of Elvis Presley. He and his mother knew the words to all of Presley's hit songs.

As a teenager, Bill loved music and practiced playing the saxophone every day. He played in his school's jazz ensemble and won first chair in Arkansas's All-State Band.

Most people in Bill's hometown belonged to the Republican Party. But Bill preferred the ideas of the Democratic Party. Kennedy was a Democrat—and Bill's hero. Bill admired the way Kennedy wanted to help all Americans, rich and poor, black and white. Before meeting the president, Bill had told his friends that when he grew up he wanted to become a doctor, a reporter, or a musician. But after attending Boys Nation, he returned to Arkansas with a new dream. "When I went home, I had the feeling that if I worked hard and prepared myself, I could have an impact," he later recalled. Bill Clinton had decided to become a **politician.**

All his life, Bill Clinton would treasure this photograph. It was taken when Clinton was in high school and had the chance to meet President Kennedy. Today, Kennedy is still one of Clinton's personal heroes.

Bill Clinton has said that he first became interested in politics during the presidential election of 1956. That year, Dwight Eisenhower won a second term as president.

One year later, he graduated from high school. He decided to attend college at Georgetown University, because it was located in Washington, DC. He wanted to live in the nation's capital city—the heart of American political life. Georgetown is a very expensive school. Clinton was able to get there only because he was awarded **scholarships** based on his good grades. He also worked part-time to help pay for school. At Georgetown, Clinton was popular and busy, just as he had been at home. His classmates thought he was bright, funny, and friendly. Twice he was elected president of his class.

CHAPTER TWO

THE YOUNG POLITICIAN

It was in college that Bill Clinton became active in politics for the first time. During the summer of 1966, he spent his summer vacation back home in Arkansas. There he took part in his first political **campaign.** He worked for Judge Frank Holt, who was running for governor of Arkansas. During Holt's campaign, Bill Clinton practiced public speaking. Holt lost the election, but Clinton's work paid off in another way. Holt helped Clinton find a part-time job back in Washington.

The job was with Arkansas senator J. William Fulbright. Fulbright was chairman of the Senate's foreign relations committee. Clinton worked for Fulbright as an aide. Much of his job was not very exciting. He sorted mail, cut out articles from newspapers, and filed papers. But at the same time he got the chance to learn about the nation's dealings with other countries.

Clinton won a Rhodes Scholarship his senior year at Georgetown University, which gave him the opportunity to study at Oxford University in England for two years. Here he is shown in 1968 while at Oxford.

Clinton was offered a scholarship to study music in college, but he decided to go to Georgetown University and study international affairs instead.

At the time, the United States was involved in the Vietnam War. Thousands of young American men were being **drafted** into the military. They were sent overseas to fight in the war, and many of them lost their lives. Fulbright firmly believed that the United States should withdraw from the Vietnam War. His opinion had a strong effect on Clinton. He did not want the United States to send any more American men to fight in a faraway country.

In 1968, during his final year in college, Clinton won a Rhodes Scholarship. Every year, only 32 students in the United States earn this prestigious honor. The winners are chosen because of their academic excellence and strength of character. Students who win the scholarship are awarded at least two years of study at England's Oxford University after they graduate from their college.

US Marines carry a wounded comrade to a helicopter during a combat operation in Vietnam in 1967. Bill Clinton went to rallies that protested the war and supported politicians who wanted to withdraw US forces from Vietnam.

Clinton studied in England from 1968 to 1970. Looking back, he remembered reading hundreds of books and arguing with his tutors about politics and foreign affairs. He grew his hair long and went to rallies to protest the Vietnam War. He found his studies challenging, but decided not to complete a degree there. Instead, he wanted to earn a law degree in the United States. So he returned to the United States to enroll at Yale Law School in

Martin Luther King Jr. was assassinated in 1968, while Clinton was going to school at Georgetown. After King's death, rioting broke out in many cities, including Washington, DC. Clinton worked with the Red Cross to deliver food and clothing to people whose homes had been burned during the riots.

New Haven, Connecticut. Yale is among the best schools in the nation. One reason he chose to go there is because he realized that attending Yale would help him meet powerful people. Knowing the right people could help him become a successful politician.

Clinton attended Yale for three years, until he obtained his law degree in 1973. In 1970, he worked on the political campaign of Joe Duffy of Connecticut, who was running for the US Senate. In the presidential election of 1972, Clinton worked for the Democratic Party's presidential candidate, George McGovern. Students around the country supported Senator McGovern because he wanted Americans to withdraw from Vietnam. Clinton managed McGovern's campaign in Texas. This was a big responsibility for Clinton, because he had to manage a large amount of money. He also organized the efforts of hundreds of volunteers. McGovern lost the election, but Clinton gained important experience from the campaign.

At Yale Law School, Bill Clinton admired a young woman named Hillary Rodham. They were in a class together, but Bill was afraid to talk to her. One day in the library, she caught him gazing at her. Hillary walked up to him and said, "Look, if you're going to keep staring at me, and I'm going to keep staring back, I think we should at least know each other. I'm Hillary Rodham."

While at law school, Clinton began to date another student, Hillary Rodham. Like Clinton, she was hardworking and wanted to achieve great things in life. They liked each other immediately. Clinton graduated with a law degree in 1973. Rodham stayed at Yale longer than Clinton did, but their friendship continued.

After law school, Clinton moved back to Arkansas. He took a job as a law professor at the University of Arkansas in Fayetteville. The following year, in 1974, he decided to run for office for the first time. He entered the election for the US House of Representatives. He lost to John Paul Hammerschmidt, the **incumbent,** but the race was close. In fact, it was the closest race of Hammerschmindt's 26 years in office. From this point on, Clinton would be popular among Arkansas Democrats.

Clinton met Hillary Rodham (shown here while a student at Wellesley College) when they were both studying at Yale Law School. The two liked each other from the start. After dating for several years, they married in October of 1975.

Hillary Rodham had moved to Arkansas to help with Clinton's campaign. She also worked as a law professor at the University of Arkansas. On October 11, 1975, the couple married. Often in his life, Bill Clinton would say how grateful he was to have Hillary as a partner. He would always admire her intellect and drive.

In 1976, Clinton's popularity among Arkansas Democrats got him elected attorney general of the state. An attorney general is the chief lawyer who works for a state or national government.

In the early 1970s, President Richard Nixon was accused of wrongdoing. Congress formed a special committee to investigate the matter, which became known as the Watergate scandal. After graduating from Yale, Bill Clinton and Hillary Rodham were both offered jobs with this congressional committee. Hillary accepted the position, but Bill decided to return to Arkansas, where he became a law professor.

After winning the election, the Clintons moved to Little Rock, the capital of Arkansas. Hillary went to work for a law firm. As attorney general, Clinton's number one goal was to help the people in his state. He created a new state office to make sure utility companies **conserved** energy. He also appeared in court to argue against a phone company's plan to increase its rates. During this time, he was able to meet important leaders in Washington. President Jimmy Carter invited the Clintons to dinner at the White House. Clinton also met with other leaders in Washington, where he talked about issues such as protecting the environment and conserving energy.

As early as 1977, Bill Clinton showed his commitment to protecting the environment. As attorney general of Arkansas, Clinton fought against the construction of a coal-burning factory, which would have polluted the air.

In 1978, Clinton was ready to try for an even more important office. Even though he was only 32 years old, he ran for governor of Arkansas and won. Governor Clinton entered office brimming with ideas. First of all, he hoped to improve the state's schools. Education had made a big difference in his life, and he wanted more young people to have the same opportunities. Clinton also wanted to create a new energy department. Its job would be to find better ways to use and conserve energy. He hoped to improve health care in Arkansas as well.

Clinton was 32 years old when he became the governor of Arkansas. At that time, he was the youngest governor in the country. He is shown here with his wife, Hillary, during his first term as governor.

Arkansas governor Bill Clinton joins President Jimmy Carter during a campaign rally for Carter in Texarkana, Texas, in 1980.

Unfortunately, Clinton ran into problems while attempting to turn his ideas into reality. The nation was in a recession. During a recession, prices rise and many people lose their jobs or cannot find work. Like other states, Arkansas had money problems. The state government couldn't pay for all of Clinton's programs. When he couldn't accomplish his goals, Clinton's popularity declined. In the fall of 1980, Bill Clinton ran for reelection as governor but lost. Some people wondered whether his political career had ended. Clinton hoped not. He went back to working as a lawyer, but he had already decided to run for governor again in 1982. To help win back his popularity, he traveled all over the state, giving speeches to the many groups that invited him. He also met with people who had helped him in earlier elections.

Bill Clinton was the youngest of all 50 governors when he was elected to the office in 1978. When he lost his bid for reelection in 1980 and had to leave office, Clinton joked that he had become the youngest ex-governor in American history.

THE VIETNAM WAR

Bill Clinton grew up during a difficult time in American history. While he was a teenager, the United States had entered the Vietnam War. In 1954, the country of Vietnam had been divided into two countries. North Vietnam was communist and wanted South Vietnam to become communist, too. The United States entered the war to assist South Vietnam against North Vietnam.

Americans argued about the war. Many believed communism was dangerous. They wanted the United States to fight against this system of government wherever it occurred. Other Americans protested against US involvement in the war. As time went by, the army drafted thousands of young Americans to fight in Vietnam. Many died there. Others returned from the war wounded or mentally scarred. In the photo above, people against the Vietnam War protest outside an army induction center (where new recruits were processed) in New York City in 1967.

As young men, Bill Clinton and his friends knew that they might be drafted. Like many other young Americans, Clinton did not like the war, and he did not want to fight. In 1969, he was drafted. Earlier, college students had been excused, rather than drafted. But now the rules had changed, and some students could be drafted. After he received his draft notice, Clinton enrolled at the University of Alabama Law School. Then he joined the university's ROTC (which stands for Reserve Officer Training Corps). The ROTC prepares students to join the military after college. Joining this group meant that Clinton would not be sent to fight overseas. But that fall, Clinton did not go to law school. He returned to England instead. By that time, it had become clear that the army would soon stop drafting soldiers.

CHAPTER THREE

PRESIDENT CLINTON

Bill Clinton was governor of Arkansas for a total of 12 years. Disappointed when he did not win reelection to the office in 1980, he ran again in 1982—and won. He also won in 1984, 1986, and 1990. (In 1986, the Arkansas governor's term was changed from two years to four.)

As governor, Clinton helped the people of his state. He greatly improved the state's schools. He also worked to strengthen Arkansas's economy. As time went by, he gained fame across the country. Leaders of the Democratic Party encouraged him to think about running for president. Some expected him to run in 1988, but Clinton decided against it.

He did, however, decide to run in 1992. He knew it would be hard to beat the incumbent, Republican George H. W. Bush. But he believed it could be done. The presidential campaign of 1992 was difficult. Many Americans were upset by rumors that Clinton had been unfaithful to his wife. The Clintons went on television and admitted that they had faced problems in the past. But they said they were happy and vowed to fight together to win the election. They also said they believed their personal life should be private. Millions of voters decided the Clintons' problems did not matter.

Bill Clinton brought many positive changes to Arkansas during his 12 years as governor.

In 1988, Clinton announced that he would not run for president in that year's election. His daughter, Chelsea, was still a young child, and he believed it was important to spend as much time with her as possible. He knew candidates spent months on the road, meeting the American people and trying to win votes.

In the months that followed, Clinton gained popularity as he spoke about what he hoped to accomplish if he became president. Many people were worried about the economy. Clinton explained how he would work to improve it. He also spoke about his ideas for a new health care system. He wanted the government to help provide quality medical care, especially for people who could not afford insurance.

In July of 1992, the Democratic Party nominated Clinton as its presidential candidate. Clinton won the election in November, surprising many people. To do so, he had to beat not just Republican president George H. W. Bush, but a third-party candidate named Ross Perot.

Bill Clinton's **inauguration** took place on January 20, 1993. He hoped to make things better for the country. Hillary Rodham Clinton made headlines early in her husband's first term. President Clinton asked her to act as one of his advisers. This responsibility was very different from those of First Ladies in the past. First Lady Clinton had helped the president create a health care plan. Once he was in office, she helped him try to persuade Congress to pass it. In the end, Congress decided it would cost the government too much money. Many felt that the plan tried to do too much, too soon.

On the night of his inauguration, President Clinton played the saxophone at one of the inaugural balls.

In 1994, elections for Congress were held. Republicans won many elections across the country. When they took office the following January, they controlled both houses of Congress, the House of Representatives and the Senate. Clinton had more problems getting **bills** passed with the Republicans in power. He fought with them over the national budget, which determines how the government spends its money. Twice Congress refused to approve the plan Clinton proposed. And twice, the government was forced to shut down because it had no money.

Chelsea Clinton was 12 years old when her father was elected president. Chelsea is shown here in 1994 playing with her cat, Socks, in the Oval Office as her father works.

Without a budget, the government cannot dispense money to its programs and its workers. Nearly 300,000 government employees were temporarily laid off. National parks and museums closed. Programs such as Social Security and Meals on Wheels had no money to operate.

When the Clinton family moved into the White House, they brought their cat, Socks. Reporters liked Socks so much, they often wrote about him. The public liked him, too. Socks was even featured in a comic strip.

Clinton blamed Congress for the shutdown. Most Americans believed he was right. He said many times that it was important for the United States to have a balanced budget, meaning that it should spend only as much as it brought in. Yet some members of Congress wanted to cut **taxes** without reducing spending. By standing up to Congress, Clinton gained the respect of many.

Even though he often fought with Congress, President Clinton did help get important bills passed during his first term. One law cut taxes for small businesses. This helped them compete against larger ones, which had to pay higher taxes. As a result, many people started new small businesses. Another was a gun control law, which made it more difficult to buy guns. Clinton hoped this would help reduce crime. Finally, the Family and Medical Leave Act stated that companies must allow their employees to take time off when they have a new baby or when a member of their family becomes ill.

Clinton signed many important bills during his first four years in office, including one in 1996 to raise the minimum wage. The minimum wage is the lowest amount of money that a person can legally be paid per hour. Here he is shown surrounded by children of minimum-wage earners as he signs the bill into law.

Strengthening America's Families

A New Minimum Wage

Clinton had success in relations with other countries as well. His most important achievement was helping to **negotiate** peace between Israel and the Palestinians. Israel, a country in the Middle East, was founded after World War II. To form Israel, land had been taken from the Palestinians and other Arabs in the region. This created terrible problems. For years, a group called the Palestine Liberation Organization fought the Israelis, trying to take back land once owned by Arabs. Clinton's peace talks didn't solve the problems in the Middle East, but many believe he came closest to achieving peace there.

In 1996, Clinton ran for reelection. This time, his Repbulican opponent was Senator Bob Dole. Ross Perot also entered the race once more. The economy was an important topic again, but there were new issues as well—including questions about President Clinton's honesty. Early in Clinton's first term, he and his wife had been accused of wrongdoing.

On April 19, 1995, a powerful bomb hidden inside a truck exploded in front of the Alfred P. Murrah Federal Building in Oklahoma City. The bomb blast killed 168 people, including 19 children. Hundreds more were injured. Timothy McVeigh, a former US Army soldier who had anti-government views, was responsible for the terrorist act. McVeigh was convicted of the crime in 1997 and executed in 2001.

Years before, they had invested money in an Arkansas company called the Whitewater Development Corporation. Other investors in the company had opened a bank that failed. Reporters wondered whether as governor of Arkansas, Bill Clinton had used his power to save the bank. A special court asked a lawyer named Kenneth Starr to look into what was known as the Whitewater scandal. But the investigation could not find evidence of wrongdoing on the part of the Clintons, and they were never charged with any crimes.

In 1993, President Clinton helped negotiate a peace agreement between Israel and the Palestinians. This historic photograph shows Clinton looking on as Israeli leader Yitzhak Rabin (left) shakes hands with Palestinian leader Yasser Arafat.

But President Clinton had another problem, too. A woman named Paula Jones **sued** him. She worked for the Arkansas state government. She said that while Clinton was governor of Arkansas, he had pressured her bosses to treat her unfairly after she refused to have an intimate relationship with him.

Neither the Whitewater scandal nor the Jones lawsuit seemed important to most American citizens. They thought Clinton was doing a good job running the government. The economy was strong, crime was down, and unemployment was lower than it had been for more than 25 years. Clinton was reelected by a large number of votes.

HILLARY RODHAM CLINTON

Hillary Rodham Clinton was an active First Lady. A smart, educated woman, she graduated from law school at the top of her class. Before her marriage to Bill Clinton, she taught law. Afterward, she began her career as a lawyer. Like her husband, she was always interested in politics. She worked on many presidential campaigns before helping her husband win the elections of 1992 and 1996. During his campaigns, she made public appearances on his behalf. She talked to Americans about the important issues of the day. Americans understood that Hillary Clinton offered her husband advice and helped him make decisions.

After he won the election in 1992, she helped him prepare to become president. Together they chose his closest advisers and the White House staff. Later, she led the committee charged with creating a national health care plan. She also helped with other important political matters. In this photo, the First Lady testifies before a Senate committee on her health care plan in 1993.

In the past, the primary duty of the First Lady was to serve as the White House hostess. More recently, First Ladies have been more involved in government. Eleanor Roosevelt and Rosalynn Carter are two First Ladies who helped their husbands make important political decisions. Hillary Rodham Clinton would take steps they never did, however. In 2000, she ran for political office, winning a seat in the US Senate.

She was reelected in 2006. In 2007, she began a history-making campaign to run for election as president of the United States, which she ended in June 2008. In December, president-elect Barack Obama appointed Clinton as his secretary of state, meaning she would be his chief adviser on foreign affairs. She was sworn into office in January 2009. In the four years she held that position, Clinton traveled more than one million miles (1.6 million km), visiting more countries than any other secretary of state.

In April 2015, she announced she would run again for president and was the Democratic presidential candidate. In November 2016, she won the popular vote 65,853,516 to 62,984,825, but she failed to win the Electoral College. Donald Trump was elected the 45th president of the United States.

CHAPTER FOUR

A SECOND TERM— AND BEYOND

In January 1997, Bill Clinton began his second term as president. He continued to work toward balancing the federal budget and improving the economy. He also wanted to improve the nation's **welfare** system.

Soon another problem would take up much of his time, however. In early 1997, lawyer Kenneth Starr announced publicly that he had begun investigating new charges against President Clinton. Rumors were

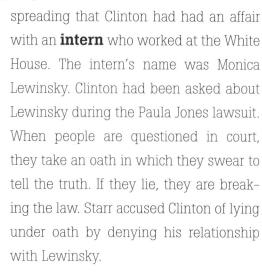

spreading that Clinton had had an affair with an **intern** who worked at the White House. The intern's name was Monica Lewinsky. Clinton had been asked about Lewinsky during the Paula Jones lawsuit. When people are questioned in court, they take an oath in which they swear to tell the truth. If they lie, they are breaking the law. Starr accused Clinton of lying under oath by denying his relationship with Lewinsky.

President Clinton's second term was clouded with accusations of wrongdoing.

Polls *showed that most Americans did not want Congress to impeach President Clinton, even though many believed he had not been completely honest with the American people. Protesters march in an anti-impeachment rally at the US Capitol to show their support for Clinton.*

On December 19, 1998, Bill Clinton became the second president in the history of the United States to be impeached. The House of Representatives charged him with lying under oath in court. Being impeached meant Clinton would be tried by the Senate.

During the trial, Americans debated about whether the president should even be on trial. The US **Constitution** says impeachment is the process used to determine whether presidents have committed "high crimes and **misdemeanors.**" Clinton's political supporters agreed that he had done something wrong in his personal life, but said that it had not affected his job as president. Those who did not support Clinton felt that he was a man of poor character and that he had broken the law by lying under oath. They believed he must be punished by being removed from office.

When Clinton was reelected in 1996, he became the first president from the Democratic Party to win a second term since Franklin D. Roosevelt 60 years before.

The American people talked a great deal about the trial. Many thought that even though President Clinton broke the law when he lied under oath, he should not be removed from office. Polls taken by newspapers and television networks revealed that people still believed Clinton was doing a good job as president. Many believed his trial was a sign of the terrible relations between Democrats and Republicans in the government.

The impeachment trial continued into February of 1999. When the Senate voted on whether to convict the president, less than half the senators voted him guilty on the **perjury** charge. This was less than the two-thirds vote required by the Constitution. Clinton remained the president. By that time, polls showed that most Americans did not consider him an honest man. Even so, he remained a popular president. Americans felt confident in his ability to lead the nation. Clinton was grateful to have a second chance.

After Bill Clinton was impeached, his approval rating was 73 percent which is very high for a president. An approval rating of 73 percent meant that out of every 100 people, 73 approved of the way he was doing his job.

After his impeachment trial, Clinton devoted most of his attention to ongoing foreign affairs. He and his aides had organized peace talks to help end a war in Bosnia, a small European country that was formerly part of Yugoslavia. He also worked to bring peace to Northern Ireland. There had been conflict there for 30 years, because some people wanted Ireland to be independent from the United Kingdom.

The economy improved during Clinton's presidency. Government spending was cut back and new jobs were created. In fact, the nation's longest period of peacetime economic growth occurred during Clinton's years in office. Here Clinton is shown in 1998, discussing the surplus in the nation's budget. A surplus means there is extra money in a budget.

Bill Clinton sent American senator George Mitchell to lead talks between the British and Irish governments. Those ended with the signing of the Good Friday Agreement in 1998.

Toward the end of Clinton's presidency, the American military became involved in a war in Kosovo, part of the Federal Republic of Yugoslavia. Enemy soldiers had invaded this tiny region. The United States and its **allies** bombed these forces to make them leave Kosovo. American soldiers then went to Kosovo as peacekeepers; none died there.

In the 1990s, Iraqi president Saddam Hussein said his country was not building dangerous weapons. He agreed to allow inspections of Iraq to prove it. But he broke his promise. In 1999, Hussein refused to let United Nations inspectors enter the country. In response, President Clinton authorized the US military to begin bombing Iraq. Iraqi weapons sites were bombed for four days.

The US Constitution says presidents can serve only two terms, so Clinton could not run for reelection in 2000. His wife, however, had decided she wanted to run for office, even while she was First Lady. She ran in New York State for the US Senate and won.

As the end of Clinton's presidency neared, he remained hard at work. He continued to work for peace in the Middle East, a goal, like other presidents, he had hoped to achieve through his presidency, but that still has not been reached. He also issued orders and signed laws that helped the environment. He did not campaign on behalf of his vice president, Al Gore, who was running for president. On Election Day, November 7, 2000, the election was so close that a winner could not be declared. It was only on December 12, after the Supreme Court ordered a stop to a recount of ballots in Florida, that Al Gore conceded the election to George W. Bush, who would follow Bill Clinton as president.

In December 2000, surrounded by schoolchildren, President Clinton signed the last budget legislation of his administration, which included the largest increase ever for the US Department of Education.

Former president Bill Clinton shakes hands with Harlem residents in July 2001, after celebrating the opening of his new office in New York following his time in the White House.

On his last day in office, January 20, 2001, Clinton issued a statement in which he admitted that he had broken the law when he lied under oath. Because of this, his law license was suspended for five years. This means he could not work as a lawyer during that time. But in exchange for his statement, officials announced that Clinton would not face another trial for what he had done.

After they left the White House, the Clintons lived in their family's new house in Chappaqua, New York. All former presidents have an office and staff, paid for by the federal government. Clinton opened his office in the Harlem neighborhood of New York City. When he left office, he was 54 years old. Later on, he told the American people that his family was deep in debt when he left the presidency. Bill Clinton earned money by publishing an autobiography and speaking at events. He became a very popular public speaker. He was paid when he appeared at events sponsored by corporations, but he also gave his time to nonprofit groups and the Democratic Party.

The Clintons had established a foundation in 1997 to raise funds for a presidential library. Eventually, however, the Clinton Foundation became a charitable organization with a bigger mission, dedicated to helping people all over the world. It has fought against the spread of AIDS in Africa and opioid addiction in the United States, and supported efforts to combat climate change.

In 2004, Bill Clinton had heart surgery after he experienced chest pain and doctors found blocked arteries. That same year, his presidential library opened in Little Rock, Arkansas. Visitors and scholars go there to view exhibits and do research. Also in 2004, the Clinton School of Public Service opened at the University of Arkansas, and the former president published his autobiography, *My Life*.

In December 2004, a massive earthquake and **tsunami** struck Asia, killing more than 200,000 people in 14 different countries. President George W. Bush asked his father, former president George H. W. Bush, and Bill Clinton to lead efforts to raise money to help the victims of this natural disaster.

In 2007, Clinton published a second book, titled *Giving: How Each of Us Can Change the World*. That year and the next, he also campaigned for his wife, Hillary Clinton, who made history by becoming the first woman ever to run for election as president of the United States. She dropped out of the election on June 7, 2008, and endorsed Barack Obama. Bill Clinton helped Obama in his campaign, and Obama went on to win the election. President Obama appointed Hillary Clinton as his secretary of state, and she served from 2009 to 2013.

Bill Clinton's autobiography, *My Life*, was a best seller. It sold over 1.5 million copies.

Former president Bill Clinton and Chelsea Clinton watch as Vice President Joe Biden swears in Hillary Clinton as the 67th US secretary of state. She was the third woman to serve in the role.

In the meantime, Bill Clinton continued to work. In 2010, he and former president George H. W. Bush worked together again, this time raising money for victims of a **devastating** earthquake in Haiti. In 2011, he published a new book, *Back to Work*, about the American economy. He campaigned for Barack Obama when he ran for a second term as president in 2012. Hillary Clinton ran for president again in 2016, and he supported her. In 2018, he published a novel, *The President Is Missing*, cowritten with the best-selling author James Patterson.

Today, Americans are frequently divided over politics, and some have a negative opinion of Bill Clinton. Still, historians point out that the American economy was strong during his presidency and give him a lot of credit for that. The end of the war in Kosovo is still seen by many as a highlight of his presidency. Speaking about both his past and his hope for the future, Bill Clinton has made it clear that he hopes he will be remembered as a great president.

Former president Bill Clinton speaks during a campaign rally for his wife, Hillary Clinton, who was the Democratic presidential candidate in the 2016 election.

WHAT IS IMPEACHMENT?

When the United States was a new nation, the men who wrote the US Constitution understood that someday a president might be involved in a crime. Or perhaps a president might do something so wrong that he or she should no longer remain in office. The Constitution gives Congress the power to:

1. Impeach the president
2. Put him or her on trial
3. Convict him or her
4. Remove the president from office

This is how the impeachment process works:

1. According to the Constitution, if a majority of members of the House of Representatives vote that they believe the president has committed "treason, bribery, or other high crimes and misdemeanors," then they have impeached the president. Three presidents have been impeached: Andrew Johnson in 1868, Bill Clinton in 1998 (whose impeachment trial is pictured above), and Donald Trump in 2019. None was found guilty of a crime. In 1974, President Richard Nixon resigned before the House voted whether to impeach him.

2. Once the House has impeached the president, the Senate must put him or her on trial. During the trial, the Senate hears evidence of the president's wrongdoing. The president's lawyers defend his or her actions. Then the senators vote. If two-thirds or more of the senators vote to convict, then the president must be removed from office. If less than two-thirds of the senators vote to convict, the president is acquitted and remains in office. (The Constitution allows Congress to impeach the vice president and other civil officers of the United States. Civil officers include judges and other important government officials.)

TIME LINE

1940	1960	1970	1980	1990

1946
William Jefferson Blythe is born on August 19. His mother is Virginia Blythe. His father, William Jefferson Blythe Sr., dies in a car accident three months before his son is born.

1963
Clinton makes his first trip to Washington, DC. As a participant in Boys Nation, he meets President John F. Kennedy.

1964
After graduating from high school, Clinton enrolls at Georgetown University in Washington, DC.

1968
During his final year of college, Clinton wins a Rhodes Scholarship. He travels to England to study at Oxford University.

1970
Clinton returns home from England and enrolls at Yale Law School.

1973
After earning his law degree, Clinton becomes a professor of law at the University of Arkansas.

1974
Clinton runs for election for the first time, hoping to win a seat in the US House of Representatives. He loses to the incumbent.

1975
Clinton marries Hillary Rodham on October 11.

1976
Clinton wins election as attorney general of Arkansas.

1978
Clinton is elected governor of Arkansas.

1980
The Clintons' only child, Chelsea, is born. Bill Clinton runs for reelection as governor but loses.

1981
Clinton starts a new job as an attorney. He spends much of his time building political support so he can run for election as governor again.

1982
Clinton is again elected governor of Arkansas.

1988
Democrats hope Clinton will run for president, but he decides against it.

1992
Clinton wins election as president of the United States, beating Republican George H. W. Bush, the incumbent.

1993
Clinton is inaugurated on January 20. He is disappointed when Congress refuses to agree to his plan for a national health care program. An investigation begins into the Whitewater scandal, a business deal in which the Clintons were involved years before. A historic peace agreement between Israel and the Palestine Liberation Organization is signed at the White House.

1994
Republicans win many elections and gain control of both the House of Representatives and the Senate. From this time on, Clinton must fight even harder to get bills passed.

1995
Clinton and Congress fight over the national budget. Clinton hosts peace talks between the groups that have been fighting in Bosnia, formerly part of Yugoslavia. A new Middle East peace agreement is signed, but fighting continues. Former US Army soldier Timothy McVeigh detonates a truck bomb in front of the Alfred P. Murrah Federal Building in Oklahoma City, Oklahoma, killing 168 people.

1996
In November, Clinton wins reelection to a second term as president.

1997
Kenneth Starr, the government's lawyer, continues to investigate the Whitewater scandal. He begins to investigate whether or not President Clinton lied under oath.

1998
New fighting breaks out in the Federal Republic of Yugoslavia when Kosovo is invaded. Iraqi president Saddam Hussein breaks his promise to let UN inspectors confirm that Iraq is not building chemical weapons and nuclear arms. President Clinton authorizes the US military to bomb Iraq. In December, Clinton is impeached on charges of perjury and obstruction of justice by the House of Representatives.

1999
The Senate tries Bill Clinton. On February 12, senators vote on whether to convict the president on the articles of impeachment. Not enough senators vote to convict Clinton, and he stays in office. After having failed to negotiate peace in Kosovo, Clinton orders the US military to join American allies in the bombing of the invaders. Bombing ends in June, when a peace plan is reached.

2000
Clinton continues to work with Israeli and Palestinian leaders to reach a peace agreement, but trouble in the Middle East continues. Having served two terms, Clinton cannot run in the November presidential election. His vice president, Al Gore, runs against Republican candidate George W. Bush.

2001
Bill Clinton leaves office when George W. Bush is inaugurated as the 43rd president on January 20. Clinton establishes the William J. Clinton Foundation, a charitable organization dedicated to helping people all over the world.

2002
The William J. Clinton Foundation launches the Clinton HIV/AIDS Initiative.

2004
Clinton undergoes successful heart surgery. His presidential library opens in Little Rock, Arkansas, and he publishes a best-selling autobiography.

2005
Clinton is named the United Nation's Special Envoy on Tsunami Recovery.

2007
Clinton publishes a book on the role of public service called *Giving: How Each of Us Can Change the World*. It becomes a best seller.

2008
Bill Clinton helps his wife, Hillary, campaign for the US presidency.

2009
Hillary Clinton is sworn in as secretary of state. Bill Clinton is named the United Nation's Special Envoy for Haiti.

2010
A massive hurricane hits Haiti in January, resulting in the deaths of more than 200,000 people.

2011
Clinton publishes the book *Back to Work*.

2014
The Clintons become grandparents when Chelsea and her husband, Marc Mezvinsky, have their first child, a daughter named Charlotte.

2016
Hillary Clinton campaigns for president again and becomes the Democratic presidential candidate. She wins the popular vote, but loses in the Electoral College.

2018
Clinton coauthors a novel called *The President Is Missing* with James Patterson.

GLOSSARY

abusive (uh-BYOO-siv): Abusive means treating someone cruelly. Clinton's stepfather was abusive.

acquitted (uh-KWIH-ted): Acquitted means found not guilty of a crime. Clinton was acquitted during his impeachment trial.

allies (AL-lize): Allies are nations that have agreed to help each other by fighting against a common enemy. In 1999, the United States and its allies bombed enemy forces that invaded Kosovo.

anesthetist (uh-NESS-thuh-tist): An anesthetist is a medical professional who specializes in giving people drugs to prevent pain during an operation. Bill Clinton's mother trained to be a nurse who assisted anesthetists.

assassinated (uh-SASS-ih-nay-tid): A person who has been assassinated has been killed by a murderer. Martin Luther King Jr. was assassinated in 1968.

bills (BILZ): Bills are ideas for new laws that are presented to a group of lawmakers. Because there were so many Republicans in Congress, Clinton had trouble getting his bills passed.

campaign (kam-PAYN): A campaign is the process of running for an election, including activities such as giving speeches or attending rallies. In the summer of 1966, Clinton took part in his first political campaign.

candidate (KAN-duh-dayt): A candidate is a person running in an election. While at Yale, Clinton worked for the Democratic presidential candidate, George McGovern.

communist (KOM-yoo-nist): A communist country is one in which all property and businesses belong to the government and the country's wealth is shared by all. During the Vietnam War, the United States sided with South Vietnam against the communist country of North Vietnam.

conserved (kun-SERVD): If people conserved something, they saved or didn't waste it. As attorney general of Arkansas, Clinton tried to make utility companies conserve energy.

constitution (kon-stih-TOO-shun): A constitution is the set of basic principles that govern a state, country, or society. The US Constitution includes laws about the impeachment process.

devastating (DEV-uh-stayt-ing): Actions that destroy something or someone are devastating. The 2010 earthquake in Haiti was devastating because it killed more than 200,000 people and caused massive amounts of damage.

drafted (DRAF-ted): When people are drafted, they are required by law to join the military. During the Vietnam War, thousands of young American men were drafted into the military.

economy (ee-KON-uh-mee): An economy is the way money is earned and spent. During his 1992 campaign, Clinton promised to improve the US economy.

impeachment (im-PEECH-ment): Impeachment is when the House of Representatives votes to charge a president or vice president with a crime or serious misdeed. Clinton was the second president to have impeachment proceedings brought against him.

inauguration (ih-nawg-yuh-RAY-shun): An inauguration is the ceremony that takes place when a new president begins a term. Clinton's first inauguration was in 1993.

incumbent (in-KUM-bent): An incumbent is the person who currently holds an elected office. Clinton lost his first election to the incumbent.

intern (IN-turn): An intern is a student who works at a job, often without pay, to gain experience. Monica Lewinsky was an intern at the White House in 1995.

misdemeanors (mis-deh-MEE-nurz): Misdemeanors are wrongful actions (such as lying under oath) that are less serious than heavier crimes (such as murder). Impeachment is the process used to determine whether presidents have committed "high crimes and misdemeanors."

negotiate (neh-GOH-shee-ayt): If people negotiate, they talk things over and try to come to an agreement. Clinton tried to negotiate peace between Israel and the Palestinians.

perjury (PUR-jur-ee): Perjury is the act of lying in a court of law while under oath. Clinton was accused of perjury during the Lewinsky scandal.

political parties (puh-LIT-uh-kul PAR-teez): Political parties are groups of people who share similar ideas about how to run a government. The Democratic and Republican parties are the two largest political parties in the United States.

politician (pawl-uh-TISH-un): A politician is a person who holds an office in government. Many people considered Bill Clinton a great politician.

politics (PAWL-uh-tiks): Politics refers to the actions and practices of the government. As a young man, politics fascinated Clinton.

polls (POHLZ): Polls are surveys of people's opinions on subjects. During Clinton's impeachment trial, polls showed that Americans still believed he was doing a good job.

resigned (ree-ZINED): A person who resigned from a job gave it up. President Richard Nixon resigned from office before the House of Representatives voted whether to impeach him.

scandal (SKAN-dul): A scandal is a shameful action that shocks the public. When the government investigated a business deal of the Clintons', it became known as the Whitewater scandal.

scholarships (SKAHL-ur-ships): Scholarships are awards of money to students to help them pay for college. Clinton won scholarships to attend Georgetown University.

sued (SOOD): If someone sued another person, they took them to court to resolve a disagreement. During the 1996 election, Paula Jones sued President Clinton.

taxes (TAK-sez): Taxes are payments of money made by citizens to support a government. Some members of Congress wanted to cut taxes without reducing spending during Clinton's presidency.

terms (TERMS): Terms are the periods of time a politician can hold a position by law. A US president's term is four years.

tsunami (tsoo-NAH-mee): A tsunami is an unusually large sea wave caused by an underwater earthquake or volcano. It can cause great destruction and take many lives. Parts of Asia were hit by a devastating tsunami on December 26, 2004.

United Nations (yoo-NY-ted NAY-shunz): The United Nations is an international organization set up to promote world peace and cooperation. In 1999, President Saddam Hussein refused to let United Nations inspectors into his country.

welfare (WELL-fayr): Welfare is aid provided by the government to poor or needy people. Clinton wanted to improve the nation's welfare system.

THE UNITED STATES GOVERNMENT

The United States government is divided into three equal branches: the executive, the legislative, and the judicial. This division helps prevent abuses of power because each branch has to answer to the other two. No one branch can become too powerful.

EXECUTIVE BRANCH

President
Vice President
Departments

The job of the executive branch is to enforce the laws. It is headed by the president, who serves as the spokesperson for the United States around the world. The president has the power to sign bills into law. He or she also appoints important officials, such as federal judges, who are then confirmed by the US Senate. The president is also the commander in chief of the US military. He or she is assisted by the vice president, who takes over if the president dies or cannot carry out the duties of the office.

The executive branch also includes various departments, each focused on a specific topic. They include the Defense Department, the Justice Department, and the Agriculture Department. The department heads, along with other officials such as the vice president, serve as the president's closest advisers, called the cabinet.

LEGISLATIVE BRANCH

Congress: Senate and the
House of Representatives

The job of the legislative branch is to make the laws. It consists of Congress, which is divided into two parts: the Senate and the House of Representatives. The Senate has 100 members, and the House of Representatives has 435 members. Each state has two senators. The number of representatives a state has varies depending on the state's population.

Besides making laws, Congress also passes budgets and enacts taxes. In addition, it is responsible for declaring war, maintaining the military, and regulating trade with other countries.

JUDICIAL BRANCH

Supreme Court
Courts of Appeals
District Courts

The job of the judicial branch is to interpret the laws. It consists of the nation's federal courts. Trials are held in district courts. During trials, judges must decide what laws mean and how they apply. Courts of appeals review the decisions made in district courts.

The nation's highest court is the Supreme Court. If someone disagrees with a court of appeals ruling, he or she can ask the Supreme Court to review it. The Supreme Court may refuse. The Supreme Court makes sure that decisions and laws do not violate the Constitution.

CHOOSING THE PRESIDENT

It may seem odd, but American voters don't elect the president directly. Instead, the president is chosen using what is called the Electoral College.

Each state gets as many votes in the Electoral College as its combined total of senators and representatives in Congress. For example, Iowa has two senators and four representatives, so it gets six electoral votes. Although the District of Columbia does not have any voting members in Congress, it gets three electoral votes. Usually, the candidate who wins the most votes in any given state receives all of that state's electoral votes.

To become president, a candidate must get more than half of the Electoral College votes. There are a total of 538 votes in the Electoral College, so a candidate needs 270 votes to win. If nobody receives 270 Electoral College votes, the House of Representatives chooses the president.

With the Electoral College system, the person who receives the most votes nationwide does not always receive the most electoral votes. This happened most recently in 2016, when Hillary Clinton received nearly 2.9 million more national votes than Donald J. Trump. Trump became president because he had more Electoral College votes.

THE WHITE HOUSE

The White House is the official home of the president of the United States. It is located at 1600 Pennsylvania Avenue NW in Washington, DC. In 1792, a contest was held to select the architect who would design the president's home. James Hoban won. Construction took eight years.

The first president, George Washington, never lived in the White House. The second president, John Adams, moved into the house in 1800, though the inside was not yet complete. During the War of 1812, British soldiers burned down much of the White House. It was rebuilt several years later.

The White House was changed through the years. Porches were added, and President Theodore Roosevelt added the West Wing. President William Taft changed the shape of the presidential office, making it into the famous Oval Office. While Harry Truman was president, the old house was discovered to be structurally weak. All the walls were reinforced with steel, and the rooms were rebuilt.

Today, the White House has 132 rooms (including 35 bathrooms), 28 fireplaces, and 3 elevators. It takes 570 gallons of paint to cover the outside of the six-story build- ing. The White House provides the president with many ways to relax. It includes a putting green, a jogging track, a swimming pool, a basketball and tennis court, and beautifully landscaped gardens. The White House also has a movie theater, a billiard room, and a one-lane bowling alley.

The job of president of the United States is challenging. It is probably one of the most stressful jobs in the world. Because of this, presidents are paid well, though not nearly as well as the leaders of large corporations. In 2020, the president earned $400,000 a year. Presidents also receive extra benefits that make the demanding job a little more appealing.

★ **Camp David:** In the 1940s, President Franklin D. Roosevelt chose this heavily wooded spot in the mountains of Maryland to be the presidential retreat, where presidents can relax. Even though it is a retreat, world business is conducted there. Most famously, President Jimmy Carter met with Middle Eastern leaders at Camp David in 1978. The result was a peace agreement between Israel and Egypt.

★ *Air Force One:* The president flies on a jet called *Air Force One*. It is a Boeing 747-200B that has been modified to meet the president's needs. *Air Force One* is the size of a large home. It is equipped with a dining room, sleeping quarters, a conference room, and office space. It also has two kitchens that can provide food for up to 100 people.

★ **The Secret Service:** While not the most glamorous of the president's perks, the Secret Service is one of the most important. The Secret Service is a group of highly trained agents who protect the president and the president's family.

★ **The Presidential State Car:** The presidential state car is a customized Cadillac limousine. It has been armored to protect the president in case of attack. Inside the plush car are a foldaway desk, an entertainment center, and a communications console.

★ **The Food:** The White House has five chefs who will make any food the president wants. The White House also has an extensive wine collection and vegetable and fruit gardens.

★ **Retirement:** A former president receives a pension, or retirement pay, of just under $208,000 a year. Former presidents also receive health care coverage and Secret Service protection for the rest of their lives.

FACTS

QUALIFICATIONS

To run for president, a candidate must
- ★ be at least 35 years old
- ★ be a citizen who was born in the United States
- ★ have lived in the United States for 14 years

TERM OF OFFICE

A president's term of office is four years. No president can stay in office for more than two terms.

ELECTION DATE

The presidential election takes place every four years on the first Tuesday after November 1.

INAUGURATION DATE

Presidents are inaugurated on January 20.

OATH OF OFFICE

I do solemnly swear I will faithfully execute the office of the President of the United States and will to the best of my ability preserve, protect, and defend the Constitution of the United States.

WRITE A LETTER TO THE PRESIDENT

One of the best things about being a US citizen is that Americans get to participate in their government. They can speak out if they feel government leaders aren't doing their jobs. They can also praise leaders who are going the extra mile. Do you have something you'd like the president to do? Should the president worry more about the environment and the effects of climate change? Should the government spend more money on our schools? You can write a letter to the president to say how you feel!

> 1600 Pennsylvania Avenue NW
> Washington, DC 20500

You can even write a message to the president at **whitehouse.gov/contact**.

FOR MORE INFORMATION

BOOKS

Ford, Jeanne Marie. *Hillary Clinton: Ground-Breaking Politician.*
Mankato, MN: The Child's World, 2018.

Klepeis, Alicia. *Understanding the Impeachment Process.*
New York, NY: PowerKids, 2018.

Mapua, Jeff. *Bill and Hillary Clinton: America's First Couple.*
New York, NY: Britannica Educational, 2015.

Mortmain, Beatrice. *Social Activism: Working Together to Create
Change in Our Society.* New York, NY: Rosen, 2018.

Rubinstein, Justine. *The Democratic Party.*
Philadelphia, PA: Mason Crest, 2019.

INTERNET SITES

Visit our website for lots of links about
William Clinton and other US presidents:

childsworld.com/links

*Note to Parents, Teachers, and Librarians: We routinely verify our web links to make
sure they are safe, active sites. Encourage your readers to check them out!*

INDEX